# Small Rain

*Barbara Crooker*

2014 © Barbara Crooker
ISBN: 978-0-944048-63-4
purple flag press is online at: http://vacpoetry.org/purple-flag/
Interior design by forgetgutenberg.com
The text is set in OFL Sorts Mill Goudy.
Cover design by Steven Schroeder.

*As always, for Richard*

# Contents

## Corvid

## Passerine

## Nectarine

*Amaryllis*

# Corvid

## After the Holidays,

the house settles back into itself,
wrapped up in silence, a robe
around its shoulders. Nothing
is roasting in the oven or cooling
on the countertops. No presents
are waiting to be wrapped, no cards
fill the mouth of the mailbox.
All is calm, all is bright, sunlight
glinting off snow. No eggnog, no Yule
log, no letters to be licked
and stamped. No more butter
cookies, no more fudge, just miles
to go on the treadmill, another round
plate added to the weight machine.
All our good intentions pave the road.
We stride out into the new year,
resolute to become firm, to define
our muscles, to tighten our borders.
The thin tinsel of the new moon
hangs in the dark sky, a comma
dividing the sentence between
last year's troubles and this year's
hopes. The calendar ruffles her pages,
a deck of shiny cards, deals out
a fresh new hand.

## Dreaming of Florida

January's endless grisaille hours, and I'm dreaming of Florida,
even though the snow keeps slanting its fitful lines, virgule
after virgule, and no two alike...Charcoal and white juncos,
beige grey doves flit from the feeder to the ground. I want something
startling, like the hot pink daiquiri of a flock of spoonbills. I want
to smell coconut tanning oil on glistening skin. Be where
egrets decorate the lawns like statuary of the rich. Where houses
are painted the colors of sherbet: lime, lemon, orange...
Citrus globes illuminate the trees, and people leave them in paper
sacks on the street with cardboard signs: *Help yourself to Florida
sunshine.* While here in the north, the sky is made out of the stuff
wadded in the neck of an aspirin bottle; bits of it slough off, drift
down like dandruff, cover the scruffy lawn.

## February Second

*The lines in italics are from*
*An Exact Replica of a Figment of My Imagination*
*by Elizabeth McCracken*
*A child dies in this book...a baby is stillborn.*


The snow is coming down again, the ground pale as Snow White's skin,
and a blood-red cardinal lands on the black lid of the barbecue,
where I've scattered some seeds. In the book I'm reading, a sentence
flies off the page, flaps between my eyes: *It's a happy life, but someone*
*is missing.* Someone is always missing. Time stopped forty years ago
in the delivery room in those last moments before the nurse
couldn't find the heartbeat. I became a watch that no longer ticks.
*You cannot change time,* but I wish I could be innocent again,
believing all stories have happy endings. *Closure is bullshit.*
You never forget, though everyone else does. Here is a birthday
unmarked on a calendar, where no cake is baked, no icing piles up
in drifts, no candles are wished on. Forever after, I am the bad fairy,
the one you don't want to invite to the christening. This story is
so sad that no one remembers it, and I have to tell it again and again.
Just like this snow, which keeps stuttering down, trying to write
its little white lies, but the black facts refuse to be swaddled;
their harsh calls rise up, crows on the snow.

## Triolet in Black and White

The crows are smoking dark cigars,
their ashes spill upon the ground,
the snow's white gauze hides burns and scars.
Those crows who smoke their black cigars—
you'd think they came in hired cars,
the way they throw their weight around.
The crows draw deep their cheap cigars,
their ashes trash the snowy ground.

## What the Raven Said

as he balanced on a branch of Douglas fir,
was that it's dark under the stars, the planet
spinning through space like the toss of a coin—
It's winter, and the currants grow sweeter
under their cover of frost. The river bears its load,
weighed down with what comes from upstream.
The season of loss, the longing for light
like sugar on cake. The form that memory
takes, straight shots from a tumbler of gin.
That was the breath of the raven, its harsh song,
movement and line, the snow, falling.

## Wings

A small day of fog and rain;
outside my window, thousands of snow geese,
their calls muffled in the low clouds,
swirl up over the ridge of the woods,
eddy in their muddled formations,
turn back on themselves, and are gone,
like the ghosts of geese, or something filed
in memory's cloud bank, a thought,
an elusive word, whose song you recognize,
but whose name can not be found.

The fog grows thick, slipping closer, editing out
the blue hills, the farmer's fields, the hedgerow,
and back path. The black arms of the cherry tree
scratch their marks on the sky's white drawing pad—
Hard to believe spring's buds lie dreaming
along the dark bark. Hard to believe summer's
cherries will dangle from these branches
in a green and leafy sky.

The cloak of whiteness unspools out of the air,
wraps around the house like a wooly shawl,
clammy and chill, all the clouds coming home
to roost, enormous white birds, tucking
us under their warm feathered wings—

## Candlemass

Whose idea *was* this, Pennsylvania in February,
month of the drear, trees bare as a politician's promise,
the landscape every shade of beige, gray, brown...
The ragged lawn's a carpet so frayed, you'd rip it up
if you could. No snow, nature's white-out, to cover things
up, fill the fields with light. Dark hills, like woodchucks
tucked in their burrows, huddle against the cold, smudge
the horizon. This is the dead space, the pause on the telephone
before the bad news. The few birds at the feeder are wearing
their shabbiest overcoats, the kinds that only come in dull
colors. Everything splashy has headed south, and it's six
more weeks til spring arrives, wearing her skimpy green dress.
What's to be done? I go to the kitchen, put on the kettle,
let it whistle, pour jasmine tea, pretend it's the sun
I'm holding cupped between my two chapped hands...

## Late February,

and light begins to soften
around the edges. Snow's flannel
sheets recede, fold back, and look,
the grass is still there,
a fresh green quilt waiting
to be hung on the line.
Crocus cut their teeth
in perennial beds.
Spring holds her breath.
White-throated sparrows
whistle up the sun.
Every day, another cup of light.

# Passerine

## Suddenly,

it's almost spring, and the new blue sky
is full of clouds, blowing and tossing
like somebody's wash, though the air's
still cold and the ground's still hard. If you
look closely, you can see buds starting to swell,
sticking their little chests out, and here are the first
stabs at green, crocus and daffodils piercing
through dirt's dark cloth. Though the finches
are still wearing their winter coats, dull
serviceable tweeds, the fields on the hills
have shifted into green, full speed ahead,
and the robins are out of the starting gate.
Everywhere, bare branches
toss in the wind, *hello, hello, hello.*

## March

Walking in the woods, thinking about the coming war,
late snow sifting down, I startled some geese
in the nearby cornfields; they took off in squadrons, bugles
blaring; the *whump, whump* of their wing beats, rotors
in the wind. I was thinking about Li Po's "Grief in Early Spring,"
and I grew colder, knowing what lies ahead, all those sons
flying off with bright fanfares, returning home in silence.

Here, the Jordan Creek cuts through the marshes, rushing
over stones, over pieces of ice. And the snow keeps on falling,
softly, lightly—the coverlet a mother might settle on a cradle,
as she watches her newborn sleep to make sure he's breathing,
his small chest still moving, up, and down.

## March

*lines 1 and 2 are quotes by Garrison Keillor*

March, the month God designed to show those
who don't drink what a hangover is like.
In my garden, the purple verb of crocuses
shoulder their way up, despite the layer
of gravel thrown by the salt truck, despite
the thick mat of dried leaves—This is the
month that finds me talking to the dead,
whose numbers increase like corms
the older I grow. Here, in the bleakness
of March, the grass is thatchy, patched
burlap. Bare witchy trees. The body's
slow decline. The right and the left
are at it again, jabber, jabber, jabber.
But into this month of drab, here comes
the crocus, sticking out its plum tongue,
inciting the woods to riot.

# Up,

up, up from the dead, the crocuses resurrect
themselves, unscroll their tiny prayer flags—
purple, white, and gold—thumb their noses
at winter. *Here we are,* they announce,
*just when you thought we weren't coming.*
Their striped leaves pierce the ground, a corona
of nails. And how the bees love them, bumbling
into their hearts, their egg-yolk stamens. Soon,
the daffodils will ring their yellow chimes,
and hyacinths will cense the air. But right now,
there's only one flower, and it's going for broke,
spilling its jar of wet paint in the perennial border,
sending up road flares, breaking out in song.

## Monday

The sky's as low as an old white shirt
someone's tossed on the line, and the snow's
been stuttering down all day, even though
the daffodils are burning, hot little suns,
and the calendar's saying *April* in just
a few days. This close to seventy,
how many springs are left on my ticket?
But up pops a cardinal, bright as a lipstick,
and he's singing something about cheer, even
as the snow comes down, erases the lawn.

## In Spring, the Sun Licks Everything Golden

Driving to a reading, three hours north, I see that the trees have retracted their leaves,
taken back their green words. No giddy ruffled cherries flirt
with the bold blue sky; here, it's a shyer, quieter shade.
The hills stretch, hazy with possibility, and daffodils have just raised
their open mouths in wonder. The green and gold dance is about to begin.

William Carlos Williams wrote, *Still, the profound change/has come upon them:*
*rooted, they grip down and begin to awaken.* I have been asleep
a long time. How can we not love this world, and everything
in it? The grass is so tender and new, it might bruise if you walk
on it, and look, there are violets where my heel touched down.

## Spring

Right now, just before green,
there's a blush on the branches
as buds flush out red, and April
holds her breath, not sure
if she wants to open the door.
The budget isn't balanced;
we teeter from crisis
to crisis. But the finches
are in their yellow slickers,
flitting from twig to twig,
and the bees are humming
quietly to themselves. The buzz
is, it's happening, whether
we're ready, or not. So strip
off your sweater. Polish
you patent leather shoes.
Butter yourself with the sun.

## Seeds

*May you be cursed by living in interesting times,*
someone famous once said, and we certainly are,
the little fires of terrorism flaring up all over,
the fear of a larger conflagration fanned
by the rumor mills, kindled by TV—
How do we live, if this day might be the last?
My new grandson is three months old; when he smiles,
it's not with his mouth, but with his entire body.
I say we need to start marching, put one foot in front
of the other. We need to sift gold from sand, truth
from image, throw the lying snakes
out in the grass. Down in the meadow, daisies
are massing in protest, and wise women
tend their herb gardens, where rockets
of purple sage and yellow loosestrife are blooming,
stamens and pistils cocked. Let's sow wildflowers,
not discord. There are eighteen different shapes
in the animal cracker zoo. The Eskimos have thirty-four
names for snow. How many ways can we wage peace?
What kind of coin are you hoarding in your pocket
to pay Charon to ferry you across?

## Passerines
*The last two lines are from Isaiah 55, v.1 and v. 12.*


This had been a difficult week, us at cross purposes,
spring lagging behind, dragging its feet, and days
on end of steady rain. The calendar said *t-shirts,*
*flip flops, sandals,* but we were hunched in sweaters,
stoking the fire. And then, and I know it was not
a miracle, the rain lifted, and the grass was a jolt
of electric green. The quarrel we were nursing
evaporated like morning mist, and there,
at the feeder, after years of trying—making
nectar, slicing oranges—was a pair of orioles, startling
as if the sun decided to fly down from the sky,
a flashy splash of citrus soda in my ordinary backyard.
*Come all you who are thirsty, come to the waters.*
*You will go out in joy and be led forth in peace.*

## Rufous-Sided Towhee

*The teaching of Zen is: drink your tea.*
*—Jane Hirshfield*


Which is what the towhee says as he
scratches in the underbrush, searching for food.
Black and white with rusty sides, he loves
the understory, the margins, the hedgerows.
He sinks into the afternoon like brown leaves
steeping in hot water. He knows no ambition
or envy, wants nothing beyond this spring day,
sunlight spreading like honey on toast. Up pops
my list, the items to check off, the errands to run,
the weeds to pull. The towhee sings again:
*Drink your tea.*

## Blocked

Late May near Charlottesville, and the Blue Ridge mountains
loaf along to my left, wrapped in their usual haze. The sky
is a blank sheet, untroubled as a baby's sleep. A cardinal
twangs his notes of cheer; he has no truck with irony and post-
modernism, and a bluebird—bluer than blue—flashes about the grass
in his cloak of sky. The twin bags of doubt and self-loathing I have
been dragging around all week start to grow lighter. A breeze gently
riffles the pages of the underbrush, and all the words I've been looking for
assemble themselves on the lawn. I just have to coax them onto paper,
the shy little darlings. But a gust of wind blows up, and they're gone.

## Le Temps Perdu

I'm sitting here in this green glade, trying to write, at a wrought iron table
patterned with roses, but I'm empty of words, a dictionary of blank
pages, a pen out of ink. Sunlight is filtering through a thousand
tiny leaves, seeping down to the grass and ivy, like sitting
in a cup of green tea. All I can do is burble mindlessly,
like the house wrens and robins, haunted by the ghosts
of what I've written here, other times. I'm sure
the Chinese philosophers have a name for this, revisiting a place
of former happiness that you can never recapture. The cardinal
keeps singing *compare, don't compare*, and a squirrel runs up the path,
cracks a nut in his sharp little teeth. Something wonderful is just about to happen.

## Dark Wings

All he wanted to do was get back home,
sit in the sun, just one more time, not die
in the hospital, alone. And my mother,
too, all she wants is to be wheeled outside
on these late days in May, low humidity,
light breeze, air full of birdsong
and the sweetness of roses. Isn't that
what heaven is? Add a wooden deck,
a few friends, chairs you can sink back in,
a flowered umbrella for shade. Something cold
to drink, the small jingle of ice cubes. Everything
soft and slow. No watches. The sun pouring down
its lemon light, the juice we used to rinse our hair in,
to make it shine like summer. And even though
night is coming, we can sit here until the stars come out,
their hard diamonds spelling stories in the sky. We can
keep on talking. We don't ever have to go in.

## Dianthus

My mother comes back as a dianthus,
only this time, she's happy, smelling like cloves,
fringed and candy-striped with a ring of deep rose
that bleeds into the outer petals. She dances
in the wind without her walker, nods pinkly
to the bluebells. She breathes easily, untethered
to oxygen's snaking vines. Lacking bones,
there's nothing left to crumble; she's supple,
stem and leaf. No meals to plan, shop for, prepare;
everything she needs is at her feet, more rich and moist
than a chocolate cake. How much simpler
it would have been to be a flower in the first place,
with nothing to do but sit in the sun and shine.

# Nectarine

## Zen

The sky is neither here, nor there, a pale
blue, few high clouds, the streak of a chalk-
board just erased—Birds busy themselves,
gossip in the hedgerow, while I doze in the shade.
The afternoon spends its gold coin. Cardinals
thread the trees, red, red, while a mockingbird
glides across the lawn, epaulets flared. The air
stretches and warms; you could pull it
like molasses taffy. I no longer have bones.
My spine fits this Adirondack chair like clay
poured in a mold. I want to be neither here,
nor there. Birds hum me to sleep.

## Loafing

All right, I'll admit it, I have just spent the afternoon watching a street gang of mockingbirds chase each other in and out of the redbud tree, the walnut, and all the low lying hedges, the winner challenging the losers to an *a cappella* sing-off, a braggadocio mix of cardinal, chickadee, rusty gate, old muffler, far-off train. They fly low, modified dragsters; you can almost see the flames stenciled on their sides. The subtext is *me! me! me!* In the bushes, the girls are unimpressed. They yawn, flick their gray and white fans, and are gone.

## Tu Wi's Picks a Dandelion, and
## Thinks About the Impermanence of Things
*Tu Wi's is an imaginary poet of the S'ung Dynasty (960-1260)*

Little suns, fallen to earth, blaze on the greening grass.
Landlords despise them, dig out their fiery pinwheels
with metal prongs, muttering words like "common"
and "weeds." Their notched leaves, jagged lion's teeth.
Their sunny faces, shaggy little manes. Old people
gather them along the roadside in early spring,
eat them in salads with hot bacon dressing
to strengthen the blood. Or distill them in flowery wine.
But most pass them by, too usual to notice.
When they go to seed, a child's breath or a puff
of wind sends thousands of tiny parachutes spinning.
They shall inherit the earth.

## Weeds

A dandelion raises its sunny face,
innocent of the war between garden
and lawn, pesticides and organic farming...
It digs in its tough roots, spreads its spade-
shaped leaves. Later, when it goes to seed,
I see the starry globe and think of my mother's
last mammogram, the dark spot the radiologist
showed us, the ductile carcinoma that had rooted
there. But she's still with us, granted the grace
of days, and I have come to push her chair,
let her feel the air on her face and arms.
She exclaims at the pink water lilies,
the field of coreopsis, the ornamental grasses
growing around the set of ponds in the place
she now calls home. Days, maybe years,
before her body gives in, and a different
kind of spade digs up the ground.

## In the Herbal Garden of Earthly Delights,

full-fat buttercups glisten, and honeysuckle
plays its siren song, sweetness on the air.
Lemon balm, lemon thyme, lemonade
all need a scoop of sugar, rock crystals dissolving
on the tongue, dangerous as methamphetamine.
What we are drawn to sometimes destroys us,
our bodies' hungers confused in the labyrinth
of advertising claims. Nobody longs
for the sharpness of chives, the pungence of sage,
the tang of oregano. No one makes them into soft drink
flavors or markets them on a flickering screen. Still,
let's hear it for the herbs; without them minced and chopped
in a stew, recipes would have no savor, without them,
our lives would be monochromes, tuneless songs,
a field of genetically modified corn stretching,
an ocean of flat bland green,
as far as the eye can see.

## Mulch
for Rosemary Winslow

Loosening is what seems to be happening,
the once taut muscles of my hamstrings
and calves letting go like an untuned
string instrument, and my belly,
stretched out four times
to become the globe, is a bowl
of pudding quivering on the shelf.
Imperceptibly, each year my breasts
lower to meet my thighs. Women
in my family lose their edges early,
grow rounder, like meatballs, chin
to bosom to stomach, as the years
roll by. Shoulders slope like the worn-
down Appalachians. Gravity
always wins. Trees exfoliate
bark and leaves; worms and beetles
turn it into duff. I breathe in,
standing as tall as my crumbling
vertebrae will let me, in Mountain
Pose, holding off, as long as I can,
the slow descent to mulch.

## Building a Compost Pile

is not unlike building a poem: making something
out of nothing, turning straw into gold, garbage into loam.
Take what others would throw out:
eggshells, apple peels, coffee grounds,
newspapers full of cumbersome verbiage,
banana skins, grapefruit rinds, grass clippings,
and add to it daily.

If it seems like nothing's happening, you're wrong.
In the dark, heat and pressure build;
things begin to break down, add up.
Turn, aerate, let it breathe. Add water.
Add worms. Add eye of newt, and bacteria.

It's earthy as a river; it smells like a stable floor.
Are those critics I hear, typing away,
or crickets in the corner of the woodpile?
How do you know when it's done?
Well, you don't, you just abandon it,
to misquote Paul Valéry.

But scoop some out—moist and dark as a chocolate torte,
black gold—this compost, this humus, it's a richness
you can never get enough of.

## Taking Down the Locust

If the builder hadn't
planted it there
in the first place—
too close to the house
and right over
a terra cotta
sewer line—
we wouldn't be doing
this today, deconstructing
the locust limb
by limb, but we are...

Paul Bunyan with
a chainsaw has just scaled
its height, and is lopping
off arms, legs, letting
them drop to the drive
where his buddy
feeds them to the shredder,
turns them into mulch.
When only the trunk is left,
he slices thick segments,
tosses them in the truck.
Maybe they'll warm
someone's February nights.

But now what remains
is what's not there—
the double-compound leaves
that filtered July suns,
the shower of gold
on the driveway each October.
The pool of shade.
What remains
is a tree of air,
where no wrens scold and scold
in the highest branches
that the wind doesn't toss,
where the sun doesn't set
down its burden of light,
where there is no black net
to snatch the moon
as it flutters by.

## This Summer Day

That sprinkler is at it again,
hissing and spitting its arc
of silver, and the parched
lawn is tickled green. The air
hums with the busy traffic
of butterflies and bees,
who navigate without lane
markers, stop signs, directional
signals. One of my friends
says we're now in the shady
side of the garden, having moved
past pollination, fruition,
and all that bee-buzzed jazz,
into our autumn days. But I say wait.
It's still summer, and the breeze is full
of sweetness spilled from a million petals;
it wraps around your arms, lifts the hair
from the back of your neck.
The salvia, coreopsis, roses
have set the borders on fire,
and the peaches waiting to be picked
are heavy with juice. We are still ripening
into our bodies, still in the act of becoming.
Rejoice in the day's long sugar.
Praise that big fat tomato of a sun.

## Nectarine

It is the marriage
of peach and plum, the crunch
of tart and sweet, nectar
of fruit without the fuzz
in your teeth. It sings
summer in the mouth.
It is the August sun, with its heavy
breath, that doesn't want to go in
for the night, that sinks reluctantly
behind the dark hills, staining
the western sky tangerine, vermilion.
But still, the heat remains.
Heft it in your hand; the firm flesh
settles in. There is no word in English
that rhymes with orange. There is no
other body that calls to mine like yours,
saying strip me, eat me, fill
my mouth with juice.

## California Poppies

Look at me, their hot orange shouts;
there is nothing this flagrant in the rest
of the garden. Little floozies,
they strip off their polyester petals one
by one, down to their bottle-green stems.
Odorless as methane in a mineshaft,
they come from California,
land of easy money and fast cars.
Jezebel would have loved their style.
After the bloom is off, their pods
coil, spring, fling hundreds of seeds,
pepper the hot wind. Watch your back,
your fingers. They burn.

## Nothing Doing

It's late summer, and I'm bored
with the ten thousand shades of green,
the humidity that's turned the air
into soup, the sun's broiler
stuck on high...The same-
ness of the days, the stickiness
of the nights. There are goldfinches
bobbing on the sunflowers; ho-hum,
ho-hum. Nothing is bubbling
up from the tropics, no trouble
is brewing in the Gulf. In Washington,
it's the same old blah-blah-blah. Two hawks
hang around the clouds in lazy circles;
they might be stitching shrouds
or embroidering lazy daisies; *c'est
tout la même chose*...Mailboxes
line up like school children,
waving their little red hands. The war
drones on and on and on. Paper
wasps build nests in the eaves.
I'm sitting here watching ice
cubes melt in a glass of cold tea.
I think it may take
forever.

## Summer, 2010

*Dear future generations:*
*Please accept our apologies.*
*We were rolling drunk on petroleum.*
*—Kurt Vonnegut*


The wine-dark sea was slick with oil.
Pelicans struggled in the viscous surf,
foamy waves clotted with tar balls,
an obscene green sheen.
Sea turtles lumbered ashore,
dragged darkness behind them.

Politicians kept spewing rhetoric
and lies. BP stations beckoned
with their sunflower logos,
but we knew better, saw
that the words of their CEO
didn't match his eyes...

The sun set each night
like a smear of mustard.
Earth's black arteries
opened, and the pressed
blood of dinosaurs,
flowed and flowed...

And we kept the lights on;
we kept on driving our overly-
large cars. The shrill
sound of drilling replaced
the cicadas, became
our new national anthem...

## Mountain

*after "The Jade Mountain" by Claire Giblin*
*acrylic, ink, pencil on gessoed paper*
*for Adrianne Marcus*


August, and the sun's burners are set on high,
cicadas shrieking at noon. My friend is leaving
this floating life, cancer's dragon claws deep
in her belly. The cold mountain lies ahead,
but there are no maps or books to guide her.
We're all walking the same jade highway.

## Down the Shore

August arrives, round as a melon
bursting with juice,
carnival nights, the lights
dancing in water that
eddies around the pier, reflects the
fat moon's shimmies, a disco
globe revolving in a dark dance
hall, where waitresses and lifeguards
in cutoffs have come to
jitterbug, looking for a
kind of
love, that summer
memories are made of,
nothing for a lifetime, just
one night, when everything's
perfect, your body firm as a peach, no
quarrels, no
running out of the car
slamming the door, just
this simmering night
under the boardwalk of stars,
velvet sand on bare feet,
waves kissing ankles, toes, tiny
x's marking the spot where
your lips finally meet, on the
zenith of summer, watermelon August.

## August Slips into a New Gear,

does a 180 on this business of accumulating light. Goes to bed early,
gets up in the dark. Is noisy: the boom box of cicadas in the trees
at noon, katydids hollering about frost at night, and underneath it all,
the high-pitched whine of insects in the fields—But there are peaches,
sweet handfuls of gold, and ripe tomatoes, blessed by the sun.
September, school books and schedules, waits just over the hill.
So let's praise the Rose of Sharon while we can, wide blue petals,
scarlet throats, the red ones with blue hearts, the double mauves,
the all-whites—Let's sing a song of daylilies, of black-eyed Susans,
of Queen Anne's Lace. Let's raise a glass to the swallows,
as they strafe the purple dusk, and give it up for the hummingbirds
flashing red and green, for the crickets tuning up in the corner,
for the goldfinches eating the sunflowers' dark hearts—

## Pears

They swing
on the tree like
golden bells; around
them, air ripens the
color of bronze. Cool
smooth skin,
impervious to touch.
Softening from the
inside out, the opposite of the
stone fruits, peaches, apricots, plums.
Their bottoms swell, hips swaying like
maracas in the autumn breeze, the smoke's
blue haze. Slip a thin knife into the skin;
cut small wedges. This is the only way you
can eat the sun. Unpicked, they'll crash
to the ground, oozing and liquid, whirl
wasps into drunkenness, melt like
early snow on the lawn.

## Les Fleurs du Mal

Shadows grow, as summer ends. Nights are colder. And the pokeberries ripen, turn
almost black, fruits of darkness, nipples of night. If you brush against them, they stain
whatever they touch. These berries hang on magenta stems, look unreal, as if a child
had mixed up his crayons. Here, too, is Deadly Nightshade—lavender flowers, clusters
of stars, so like a tomato, so not. And Datura, Jimsonweed, its huge white flower
the horn of an old phonograph, the one the dog has an ear arched to listen
to his master's voice. They are common in wastelands, they flourish in hedgerows
and untilled fields. Consider the lilies of the etc. They toil not, in their damask skin.
Now it is *le crépuscule du soir*, and Baudelaire is dreaming of new flowers
in the blossoming dusk: Swollen Bladderwort, Gall-of-the-Earth, One-Flowered
Cancer Root, Nits-and-Lice, Stinking Groundsel, Trailing Wolfsbane, Common
Skullcap, Fly-Poison, Death Camas, Carrion Flower.

# Amaryllis

## Small Stanzas in Autumn

*Autumn returns, and again we are cast thistledown together*
*on the winds,* wrote Tu Fu in 755 AD, and I feel the cold air

blowing, the years falling by like so many yellow leaves.
Down in the meadow, some larkspur, a few black-eyed Susans

still bloom, but it's late in the season, everything
going to seed. The afternoon sun licks strips

of gold on my arms. A drowsy silence, hummed
by bees. The thunk of an apple, finally ripe, falling.

We tilt at the balancing point, between summer's too-much
and winter's not-enough; the sumac flickers red in the hedgerow.

Last sweet raspberries. The old cherry tree turning orange
peach orchid gold, a sunset of leaves. Small sulphur butterflies

dance on the lawn. Who could paint a sky this blue?
The pages of my notebook flutter in the breeze.

## Now

What can I say, now that summer's gone, with the weight of its heat,
its thick blanket of humidity, the cacophony of zinnias, marigolds, salvia?
Now the sky is clear blue and cloudless, that sure one-note
that can only mean October. You're gone. The leaves turn gold
in the calendar's rotisserie, giving up their green, and the burning bushes
have ignited, struck their book of matches. It's enough to make the heart break,
isn't it? We keep going down the one road, there's no turning back.

## And Now it's October,

the golden hour of the clock of the year. Everything that can run
to fruit has already done so: round apples, oval plums, bottom-heavy
pears, black walnuts and hickory nuts annealed in their shells,
the woodchuck with his overcoat of fat. Flowers that were once bright
as a box of crayons are now seed heads and thistle down. All the feathery
grasses shine in the slanted light. It's time to bring in the lawn chairs
and wind chimes, time to draw the drapes against the wind, time to hunker
down. Summer's fruits are preserved in syrup, but nothing can stopper time.
No way to seal it in wax or amber; it slides though our hands like a rope
of silk. At night, the moon's restless searchlight sweeps across the sky.

## Surfeit

Each fall, the leaves turn the color of money, copper,
bronze, gold, and then the trees go for broke, spend
it all, blow everything they've got upon the lawn.
They don't play it safe, invest in mutual funds, CDs.
Their pockets empty, they shrug, bare-limbed,
knowing the odds, that equinox will spin around
once more, and that, like magicians, they'll pull
green silk from every twig. But right now,
on the brink of winter's Great Depression,
they shrug on gray overcoats, tan fedoras, settle in
for the long night. The cards are in their favor
if they can just be patient, wait out the dry spell,
the deep freeze. Eventually, the wind will come back
from the south; if you listen, you can hear the rustle
of money in the invisible leaves.

## Blue and Gold October,

*The rooks and I rejoice not to be mute.*
*—William Matthews, The Rookery at Hawthornden*


and the air is ripe with noise: squirrels shuffling through the duff, the high chirp
of the chipmunk as it streaks through the leaves, the discordant choir of birdsong.
Even the sunlight makes music, falling in solid chords of gold on the ground.
Up in the pines, a nuthatch calls, *Why are you here, Why are you here*
down in the woods, while the rest of the world works on? Not making any money,
not punching any clock, idling the afternoon away? I settle back in my canvas sling,
let my pen stutter across the page, adding my words to the ragtag chorus,
the last notes of the year.

## Over Sixty

Well, I'm not going to give it up, not yet; love, I mean,
the horizontal disco that twists the sheets under the moon's
hot glitter dome— Yes, my leg bones ache and grind
in their sockets, and you have four long scars
where skin cancers bloomed. It takes a little longer
to get the fire going, a little blowing on the spark,
more kindling, stroking, stoking. The dogwood tree,
berries and leaves red as blood, outside my window
has burst into fire; why can't I?

## Letter to Gail

You write, "Where has the fall fallen?"
and how time is escaping, leaking like a hiss
from a blue balloon. Outside, the sky
is that lapidary azure of mid-October.
You rush from meeting to board room,
while each day the leaves shift
in color and tone, red-orange, green-gold.
When you turn, they've already fallen.
You write that you would like to stop working,
but phone messages and faxes pile up on the floor.
This air, so cold and clean you could bite it,
like an apple. All of our stories have the same ending.
Still, we drone on, little bees, drive while listening
to voice mail, drinking take-out coffee, trying to do
too many jobs in too few hours. You say you'd like to wake
up in the light, go for long walks with the dog, not answer
the phone for months. Outside the window, the unreachable
sky, the burning blue fire.

## October Strikes

a bell, and the world rings: gold, gold.
Nights grow blacker, colder.
What should we do
with the hour we've saved?
Let it collect interest
in the bank; add it to our IRAs.
Will it pay us a dividend in the afterlife?
Now frost chimes the hour,
rimes the wheat fields.
Time to turn over
the garden, to bring in
the houseplants, the wicker furniture.
Time for apples to burn, for pumpkins
to fill in their outlines, grow round
as that old silver nickel, the moon.
The sycamore leaves rattle
and cackle in the wind; it's time
to get down to the bones.
Small white ghosts
float down the street,
and we will slip
handfuls of candy corn
in their pillowcases
to keep away the dark.

## It's Monday Morning,

mid-November, the world turned golden,
preserved in amber. I should be doing more
to save the planet—plant a tree, raise
a turbine, put solar panels on the roof
to grab the sun and bring it inside. Instead,
I'm sitting here scribbling, sitting on a wrought
iron chair, the air cold from last night's frost,
the thin sunlight sinking into the ruined
Appalachians of my spine. I know it's all
about to fall apart; the signs are everywhere.
But on this blue morning, the air bristling
with crickets and birdsong, I do the only thing
I can: put one word in front of the other,
and see what happens when they rub up against
each other. It might become something
that will burst into flame.

## November

This tufted titmouse at the feeder, all perky peak and bright eyes,
is the mirror image of the sky overhead, breast of gray feathers,
orange smear of sun going down behind the clouds. Even though
the oily sunflower seed is low, he keeps coming back, ever
hopeful. The leaves have flown from most of the trees; it's
November, season of less. A long freight rattles south,
pulls the cold air behind it. The flowers have folded
their bright tents, gone back to the darkness from where
they came. Even the light leaves easily, as night closes
the cover of its dull book, draws the curtains, lowers the shades.

## At the Last Chance Saloon

The moon's a half dollar tossed on the bar,
somebody's loose change. The cold gin in the Dipper
shimmers. We seem to think we can spend it all,
that our resources will endlessly replenish, as profligate
as stars in the sky's deep pocket. But the ice caps
are melting, the permafrost is thawed, oil reserves
sucked dry, while we turn our backs on energy
harvested from sun and wind. No winners
here. Pile on the down quilts. The days grow shorter.
Turn up the thermostat, open the window. Now,
while we've got it, let everything burn.

## Sustenance

The sky hangs up its starry pictures: a swan,
a crab, a horse. And even though you're
three hundred miles away, I know you see
them, too. Right now, my side
of the bed is empty, a clear blue lake
of flannel. The distance yawns and stretches.
It's hard to remember we swim in an ocean
of great love, so easy to fall into bickering
like little birds at the feeder fighting over proso
and millet, unaware of how large the bag of grain is,
a river of golden seeds, that the harvest was plentiful,
the corn is in the barn, and whenever we're hungry,
a dipperful of just what we need will be spilled. . . .

## Nativity

In the dark divide of mid-December
when the skies are heavy, when the wind comes down
from the north, feathers of snow on its white breath,
when the days are short and the nights are cold,
we reach the solstice, nothing outside moving.
It's hard to believe in the resurrection
of the sun, its lemony light, hard to remember
humidity, wet armpits, frizzy hair.
Though the wick burns black and the candle flickers,
love is born in the world again, in the damp
straw, in some old barn.

## Nativity

The amaryllis bulb, dumb as dirt,
inert, how can anything spring
from this clod, this stone,
the pit of some subtropical,
atypical, likely inedible fruit?
But it does: out of the dark
earth, two shoots, green
flames in December,
despite the short days,
the Long Night Moon
flooding the hard ground.
Nothing outside grows;
even small rodents
are burrowed in
the silent nights.

Then, one morning—
a single stalk,
then a bud
that swells, bells
full sail, full-bellied,
the skin grows thin,
tighter, until it splits:
heralds the night
will not be endless,
that dawn will blossom,
pearly and radiant,
and two white
trumpets unfold, sing
their sweet song,
their Hallelujah chorus,
sing carols in the thin cold air,
and our mouths say O and O and O.

## About the Author

Barbara Crooker is the author of five previous books of poetry: *Radiance*, winner of the 2005 Word Press First Book Award and finalist for the 2006 Paterson Poetry Prize; *Line Dance* (Word Press, 2008), winner of the 2009 Paterson Award for Excellence in Literature; *More* (C&R Press, 2010); *Gold* (Cascade Books, 2013); and *Selected Poems* (FutureCycle Press, 2015). Her writing has received a number of awards, including the 2004 WB Yeats Society of New York Award (Grace Schulman, judge), the 2003 Thomas Merton Poetry of the Sacred Award (Stanley Kunitz, judge), and three Pennsylvania Council on the Arts Creative Writing Fellowships in Literature. Her work appears in a variety of literary journals and anthologies, including *Common Wealth: Contemporary Poets on Pennsylvania* and *The Bedford Introduction to Literature*. She has been a recipient of fellowships and residencies at the Virginia Center for the Creative Arts; the Moulin à Nef, Auvillar, France; and The Tyrone Guthrie Centre, Annaghmakerrig, Ireland. Her work has been read many times on *The Writer's Almanac*, and she has read her poetry all over the country, from Portland, Oregon to Portland, Maine, including The Calvin Conference of Faith and Writing, The Austin International Poetry Festival, Glory Days: A Bruce Springsteen Symposium, the Library of Congress, and the Geraldine R. Dodge Poetry Festival.

# Acknowledgements

*Adanna:* "Blue and Gold October,"
*American Society (FutureCycle Press):* "Summer 2010"
*Bhutan Today (Bhutan):* "Le Temps Perdu"
*Blueline:* "Les Fleurs du Mal"
*Bryant Literary Review:* "What the Raven Said"
*The Buddhist Poetry Review:* "Monday," "Sustenance"
*Canary:* "Loafing," "And Now it's October"
*Capper's:* "Late February,"
*Confluence:* "Nativity"
*Crab Creek Review:* "Over Sixty"
*The Cresset:* "March," "Up"
*The Fifty-Five Project:* "Passerines"
*For Poetry:* "Letter to Gail"
*Fourth River:* "Weeds," "Mulch"
*Gargoyle:* "Dreaming of Florida"
*Gastronomica:* "Nectarine"
*The Healing Muse:* "February Second"
*Heavy Bear:* "Zen"
*Hunger Enough: Living Spiritually in a Consumer Society (Pudding House Publications):* "Building a Compost Pile"
*Journey to Crone (Chuffed Buff Books)(UK):* "California Poppies"
*Kaleidowhirl:* "Small Stanzas in Autumn"
*Kansas City Voices:* "It's Monday Morning"
*Levure littéraire (France):* "Mountain"
*Little Pauxtent Review:* "Rufous-Sided Towhee"
*Louisiana Literature:* "Dianthus"
*Mezzo Cammin:* "Down the Shore"
*The Midwest Quarterly:* "August Slips into a New Gear"
*New Works Review:* "Wings," "This Summer Day," "Nothing Doing,"
*Parting Gifts:* "Taking Down the Locust"
*The Paterson Poetry Review:* "In Spring, the Sun Licks Everything Golden," "Blocked"
*Perspectives:* "Tu Wi's Picks a Dandelion, and Thinks About the Impermanence of Things," "November"
*Platte Valley Review:* "Now"
*The Same:* "Dark Wings"
*Santa Fe Broadsides:* "Seeds"
*Ship of Fools:* "Suddenly"

*Sow's Ear:* "October Strikes"
*Tattoo Highway:* "Pears"
*Verse Wisconsin:* "Triolet in Black and White," "Surfeit"
*Watershed:* "Candlemass"
*Wild Goose:* "March," "Spring"
*Windhover:* "After the Holidays," "Nativity"
*Women Writers:* "In the Herbal Garden of Earthly Delights,"

"March" won the 2004 Divided We Stand poetry contest. "Tu Wi's Picks a Dandelion, and Thinks About the Impermanence of Things" won the 2007 Eco-Poetry Contest for the Philly GreenFest. "Surfeit" was also part of the Jawbreaker Poetry Project, the Poetry Jumps Off the Page Verse-O-Matic. "October Strikes" won the 2004 Tall Grass Writer's Guild Poetry Prize, and appeared in their anthology, *Things That Go Bump.* "It's Monday Morning" received a 2011 Pushcart Prize nomination. "Small Stanzas in Autumn" received a Best of the Net nomination. "Late February," "Suddenly," and "This Summer Day" also appeared in *Garden Blessings* (Viva Editions). "August Slips into a New Gear" also appeared in *The Midwest Quarterly's* 50th anniversary anthology.

Many thanks to the Virginia Center for the Creative Arts for the gift of space and time, and to Barbara Reisner, Kathleen Moser, Geri Rosenzweig, Ken Fifer, and Marjorie Stelmach for their help with earlier drafts of these poems.

CPSIA information can be obtained at www.ICGtesting.com
Printed in the USA
LVOW03s0233100315

429899LV00016B/369/P

9 780944 048634